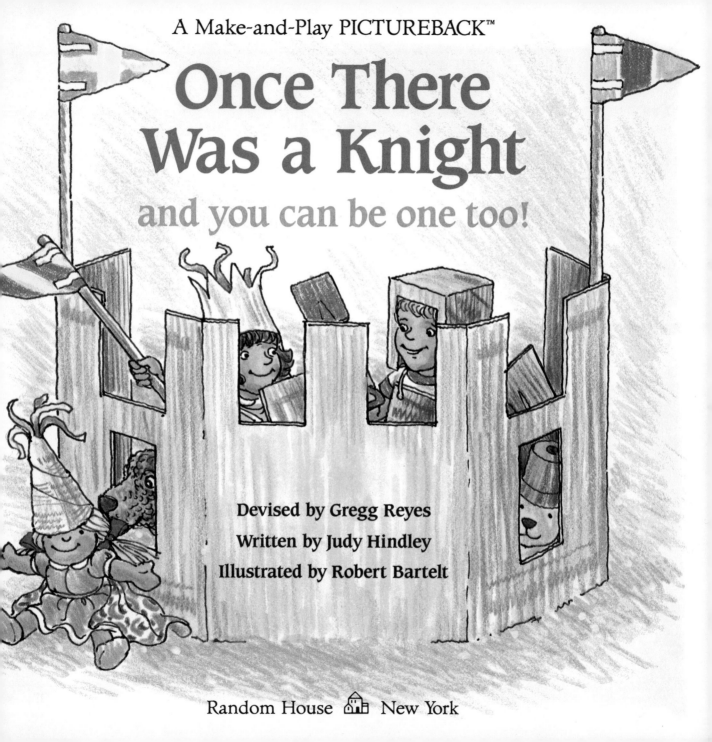

A Make-and-Play PICTUREBACK™

Once There Was a Knight

and you can be one too!

Devised by Gregg Reyes

Written by Judy Hindley

Illustrated by Robert Bartelt

Random House 🏠 New York

For all our parents,
especially Virginia

First American Edition, 1988.
Text copyright © 1987 by Gregg Reyes and Judy Hindley. Illustrations copyright © 1987 by Robert Bartelt. All rights
reserved under International and Pan-American Copyright Conventions. Published in the United States by Random
House, Inc., New York. Originally published in Great Britain by William Collins Sons & Co. Ltd., London, in 1987.

Library of Congress Cataloging-in-Publication Data:
Reyes, Gregg. Once there was a knight, and you can be one too! (A Make-and-play pictureback)
SUMMARY: Two children playing knights have wonderful adventures as they vanquish an ogre and become king and
queen. Instructions are included for making a castle, dragon, throne, etc., from cardboard and other household
materials. [1. Play—Fiction. 2. Knights and knighthood—Fiction. 3. Handicraft] I. Hindley, Judy.
II. Bartelt, Robert, ill. III. Title. IV. Series.
PZ7.R33024Op   1988   [E]   87-20485   ISBN: 0-394-89007-8 (pbk.); 0-394-99007-2 (lib. bdg.)

Manufactured in the United States of America   1 2 3 4 5 6 7 8 9 0

119002

Once

there was

3

a bold,
brave
knight!

But he was lonely.
How he longed
for a trusty knight-companic

THEN...

Once upon a time
there was another knight.
These two knights
decided to be comrades.
They promised
to be loyal friends
forever.

Their names were
Sir Fearless
and Sir Joyous.

When misfortune came
they always
helped each other.

When good fortune came
they always shared it.

8

These two knights
prepared some
shining armor

and went in search
of glorious adventures

(always followed
by their faithful servant).

They rode through
a dark and gloomy forest.

They rode past
a swift and shining river.

They climbed steep mountains
and they saw strange cities.

Everywhere they went
they did good deeds
and gathered followers,

until the time came
when they had to part.

"Farewell!" cried Sir Fearless.
"Farewell!" cried Sir Joyous.
"Blow this horn
if you should ever need me."

Alone through the forest
went Sir Fearless.
At last he came upon...

a helpless prisoner!

Should he fly to rescue
this fair maiden?

While he stood amazed
and wondering,
from a dark cave...

came a
HIDEOUS DRAGON!

Sir Fearless knew
the time had come
for action.

16

He blew one blast
upon his magic horn.

Tara-tara-tara!

17

"Courage!" cried Sir Joyous.
"I bring friends!"

"Let's fight!"
cried the dragon.
So they fought.
There was a fearsome, frightful
noise of battle.
Thunk!
went the weapons of the knights.
Thwack!
went the dragon's loathsome tail.
But nothing scared
the brave and fearless knights...

...and soon the hideous dragon
begged for mercy.
"Spare me! Help!
Release me!" cried the dragon.

"Take my castle!
Take my treasure!
Let me go!"
The dragon promised
to be good forever.

That same day
there was a great feast
and a tournament.

And these brave knights
became the king and queen!

23

BUILDING CASTLES

In a pinch, the kitchen table can be turned into a perfectly satisfactory castle—if it's raining, for example, or if you have no backyard. You could drape an old sheet over it, pin or tape a strip of cardboard battlements around the top, even place four small boxes at the corners, to be watchtowers. (Stack a few books inside to prevent the towers from toppling.)

But children love to make their own large castles, forts, and hideouts. So here are tips for making these more durable and authentic-looking. For easier storage, find some boxes that will stack inside each other. Fastening with pipe cleaners or twist ties is a helpful technique for building—at the end of the day you just undo the fasteners, take down the castle, and stack it all away for another day.

Cutting cardboard is easy if you score it and brush it with water first. To score, make a deep scratch to weaken the cardboard. Use a knife, a scissors-point, or even your fingernail, and steady it with a ruler for a straight line. Then brush water over the line, using a small watercolor brush. With patience, you can soften it so much a child can "cut" it with a ruler, or push a finger through to make a hole.

Adults should help when scissors or any other sharp tools are used. And remember, cardboard is paper, so keep it away from fire.

To make the gatehouse

Cut out two facing doors from the biggest box. Fold one down for the drawbridge. Cut the other out completely (it can be a shield). If you thread some string through the drawbridge and up through the box, the drawbridge can be pulled up. To lock it, pull the strings through the two far battlements (upended flaps), securing them in cuts made in a glued-down flap above the opposite door, as shown at far right. To make the battlements at the top, cut out middle sections from the flaps and use them to brace the remaining sections upright by taping them to the inside corners.

Brace the flaps up.

Knot the string.

Snip and glue down this flap.

Cut out sections.

Fold down.

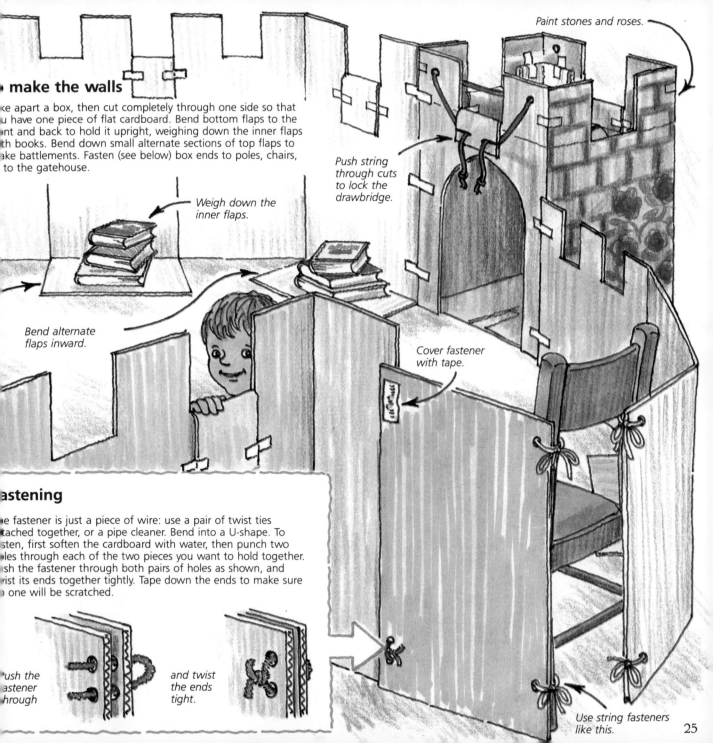

Paint stones and roses.

make the walls

ke apart a box, then cut completely through one side so that
u have one piece of flat cardboard. Bend bottom flaps to the
nt and back to hold it upright, weighing down the inner flaps
th books. Bend down small alternate sections of top flaps to
ake battlements. Fasten (see below) box ends to poles, chairs,
to the gatehouse.

Weigh down the
inner flaps.

Push string
through cuts
to lock the
drawbridge.

Bend alternate
flaps inward.

Cover fastener
with tape.

astening

e fastener is just a piece of wire: use a pair of twist ties
tached together, or a pipe cleaner. Bend into a U-shape. To
sten, first soften the cardboard with water, then punch two
les through each of the two pieces you want to hold together.
sh the fastener through both pairs of holes as shown, and
ist its ends together tightly. Tape down the ends to make sure
o one will be scratched.

ush the
astener
hrough

and twist
the ends
tight.

Use string fasteners
like this.

25

TO MAKE A HORSE OR A DRAGON

The dragon's head is bigger—a child's head must fit through a hole on the underside, to look out through the eyes. Also, a dragon has jagged teeth. To make snapping jaws, thread a long rubber band through holes in the upper and lower jaws. Knot the ends or secure them fastener-style with a cardboard tab, as shown.

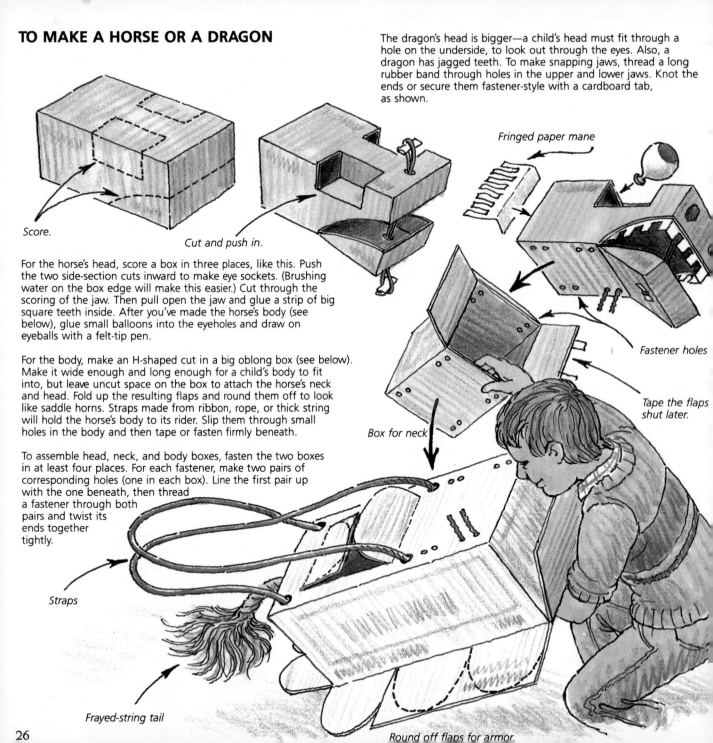

Score.

Cut and push in.

Fringed paper mane

Fastener holes

Tape the flaps shut later.

Box for neck

Straps

Frayed-string tail

Round off flaps for armor.

For the horse's head, score a box in three places, like this. Push the two side-section cuts inward to make eye sockets. (Brushing water on the box edge will make this easier.) Cut through the scoring of the jaw. Then pull open the jaw and glue a strip of big square teeth inside. After you've made the horse's body (see below), glue small balloons into the eyeholes and draw on eyeballs with a felt-tip pen.

For the body, make an H-shaped cut in a big oblong box (see below). Make it wide enough and long enough for a child's body to fit into, but leave uncut space on the box to attach the horse's neck and head. Fold up the resulting flaps and round them off to look like saddle horns. Straps made from ribbon, rope, or thick string will hold the horse's body to its rider. Slip them through small holes in the body and then tape or fasten firmly beneath.

To assemble head, neck, and body boxes, fasten the two boxes in at least four places. For each fastener, make two pairs of corresponding holes (one in each box). Line the first pair up with the one beneath, then thread a fastener through both pairs and twist its ends together tightly.

rdboard ears

Cardboard tab

per tongue

Remember

Always make sure the fastener ends point outward. Tape them
down to ensure that no one's face is scratched.

*Fasten the spine
to the head.*

Fasten together.

make the dragon's spine

apart and cut open a box. Cut the flaps into spikes, as
wn. Fasten more boxes onto it to make it as long as you like.
en the edge of the spine firmly to the head and glue or
en the spine to an old sheet to cover the person or persons
erneath.

Rubber band

*Pull the tab
to make the
dragon snap!*

Rope reins

*Heavy-duty work gloves
with cardboard claws make
excellent dragon's paws.*

MAKING ROYAL ROBES AND SHINING ARMOR

You can use cardboard to make breastplates, shields, and greaves (plate armor for the legs). Layers of old nightgowns or long skirts make wonderful robes. Remember, it's often the tiny detail that's most important—like a belt for the sword, or a splendidly jeweled brooch. (See pages 29 and 32.)

Cover armor with tinfoil to make it look like metal—or use metallic paint for a real transformation (though it needs to be kept well out of the reach of toddlers).

But never forget the power of suggestion. Everything doesn't have to look just right. After all, perhaps the invincible armor is secretly hidden underneath that T-shirt. Or perhaps it's the power of a witch's spell that makes your royal robe look like a towel…

To make swords, use a wrapping paper or paper towel roll. Tape foam rubber or several cotton balls to the end of your paper sword to make sure it won't hurt anyone.

For a long lance, roll up overlapping sheets of newspaper and tape up tightly. Fold a piece of cardboard into a cone shape—this will be the hand guard. Cut a hole in the tip to push the lance through. Remember to cover end with foam or cotton.

The battle-axe is wonderfully squashy. It's just a big sponge taped to a paper towel roll.

Armor

Attach cardboard breastplate and back plates with string fasteners, then cover with cardboard strips to place over shoulders. Tinfoil containers add impressiveness—attach with strips of double-sided tape.

A little box, with two sides scooped out so it rests comfortably on a child's head, makes a perfect helmet. For a plume, stick a tissue in a toilet paper roll. Use plenty of masking tape to stick it on.

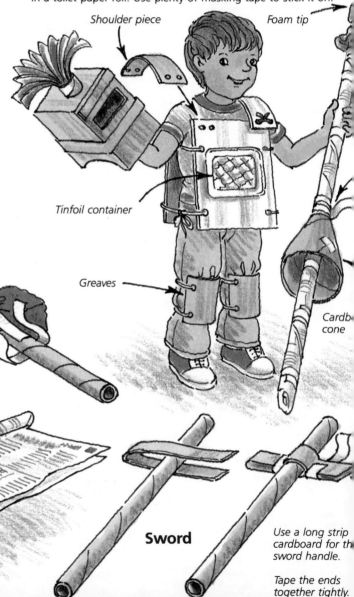

Shoulder piece

Foam tip

Tinfoil container

Greaves

Cardboard cone

Battle-axe

Long lance

Roll together to make lance.

Sword

Use a long strip of cardboard for the sword handle.

Tape the ends together tightly.

hain mail

astic six-pack holders from soda cans make amazing chain mail.
u will need ten of them to make this coat. Join them with
pe. Then fasten the sides together.

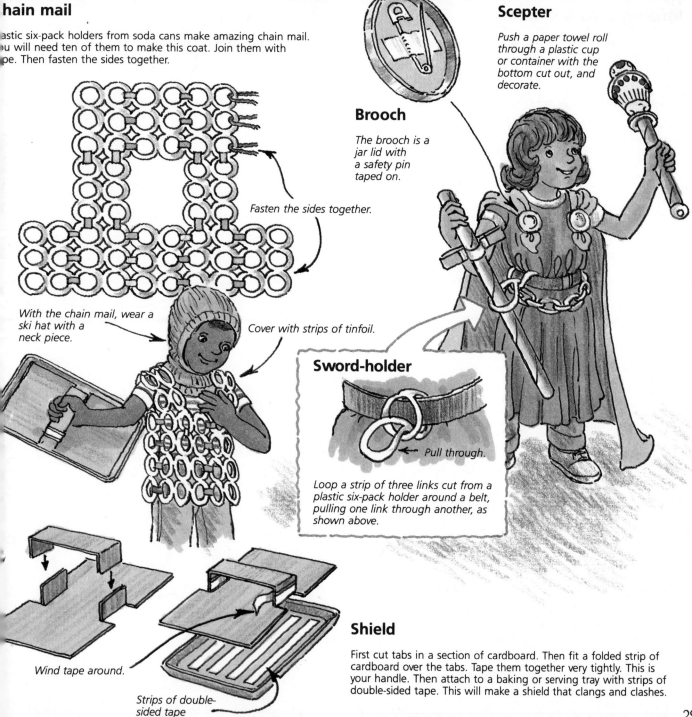

Fasten the sides together.

With the chain mail, wear a
ski hat with a
neck piece.

Cover with strips of tinfoil.

Brooch

The brooch is a
jar lid with
a safety pin
taped on.

Scepter

*Push a paper towel roll
through a plastic cup
or container with the
bottom cut out, and
decorate.*

Sword-holder

← Pull through.

Loop a strip of three links cut from a
plastic six-pack holder around a belt,
pulling one link through another, as
shown above.

Wind tape around.

Strips of double-
sided tape

Shield

First cut tabs in a section of cardboard. Then fit a folded strip of
cardboard over the tabs. Tape them together very tightly. This is
your handle. Then attach to a baking or serving tray with strips of
double-sided tape. This will make a shield that clangs and clashes.

HOLDING A TOURNAMENT

The whole point of a tournament is to show off your skills. Knights gather together, camping in tents, to have races and contests and mock battles where they can be as noisy as they like. The king and queen and all their royal court dress up as splendidly as possible. They may reward the winners of the games with treasure....

Banners, tents, and thrones make things look like a tournament—the games can be invented as you go. Children can have fun bashing each other with sponge battle-axes (see page 28), and baking-sheet shields make a satisfying *clash*! The lances are great for a game of Knockout Boxes.

Knockout Boxes

The aim is to knock the target box out of the middle so that the little box falls down into the one below. How many times can you do it without missing? Take turns and see.

before

after

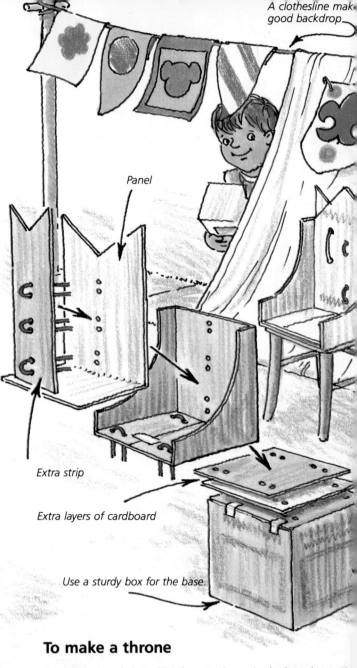

A clothesline makes good backdrop.

Panel

Extra strip

Extra layers of cardboard

Use a sturdy box for the base.

To make a throne

Cut out a curved shape like the one shown in the box above. Fix it to another box, or a chair. You can fasten or tape two boxes together to keep them steady, or fasten a box to a chair-back. Lengthen the back of the throne with an extra cardboard panel fastening another strip on for effect.

Pavilion

Throne canopy

Weigh down
with books
on the inside,
or peg down.

ther building
chniques

ore ideas for making large structures like these can be found in
nce *There Was a House.*

Flags and banners

A bright-colored emblem stitched or glued to an old towel will
transform it instantly into a banner. Try these shapes cut from
folded cloth or paper.

Fold and cut.　　　*Unfold the pieces.*

FINDING TREASURE

Look for anything that shines and sparkles—bottle caps and shiny lids, foreign coins, cheap costume jewelry, even nuts and bolts. Add seashells and pebbles painted in deep, bright colors.

For brooches, crowns, etc., cover cardboard with a thick base of modeling clay. Then you can decorate it with big white beans and pasta shapes, or noodles, lentils, cake decorations—even nuts and bolts from a toolbox. To stick noodles onto a metal lid, first cover the metal with masking tape, for a better bond.

For a really magical effect, spray the finished products with metallic paint—it looks spectacular. But take care that toddlers can't get at the paint or put the "jewelry" into their mouths. It could be harmful.

Ribbon ring

Fill a circle-shaped pasta with glitter, and press into modeling clay base. Attach to ribbon.

Painted pasta shapes

Goblet

Cut the tops from two same-sized plastic bottles. Tape them tightly together with electrical tape. Cover the bottle edges with masking tape.

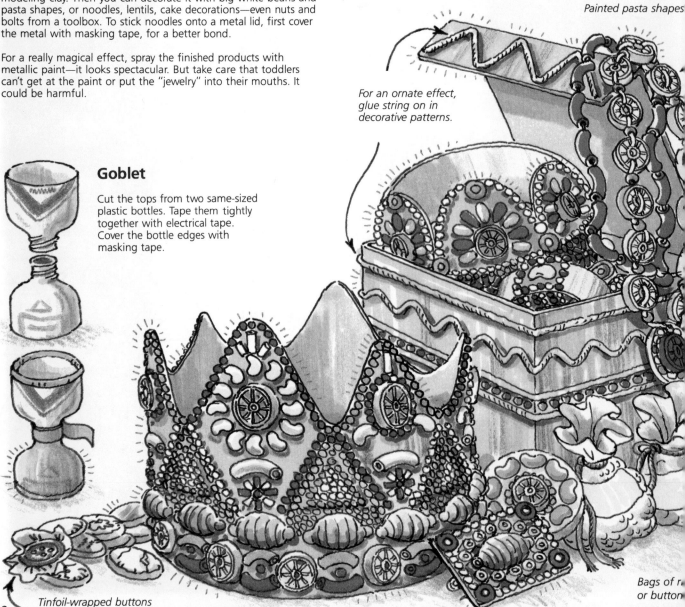

For an ornate effect, glue string on in decorative patterns.

Tinfoil-wrapped buttons or chocolates

Bags of r... or button...